What Do Lutherans Believe About *Baptism?*

John T. Conrad

CSS Publishing Company, Inc., Lima, Ohio

Copyright © 2000 by
CSS Publishing Company, Inc.
Lima, Ohio

For more information about CSS Publishing Company resources, visit our website at www.csspub.com.

ISBN 7880-1769-1   PRINTED IN U.S.A.

Lutheran Beliefs
On The Bible And Baptism

Why Start With The Bible As A Whole?

Imagine yourself sitting in on the last third of a movie. The people are laughing at certain scenes. They are glued to the screen because they know what has happened. You feel like you are "out to lunch." Now imagine what it would be like to view only one minute of one scene. Would you be surprised if it didn't make any sense? Imagine the hundreds of creative stories that could be "spun" from just that one small slice. This is what it would be like to try to understand baptism without looking at the Bible as a whole. Only within the context of the story of the Bible as a whole does it make sense. Out of context, it is subject to real misinterpretation.

God Chooses Us

The story of baptism does not begin with baptism. It begins with Abraham and Sarah in the book of Genesis. In Genesis 17, we read how Abraham was to become the "father" of a very special "family." *"This is my covenant, which you shall keep, between me and you and your offspring after you: Every male among you shall be circumcised. You shall circumcise the flesh of your foreskins, and it shall be a sign of the covenant between me and you. Throughout your generations every male among you shall be circumcised when he is eight days old ..."* (Genesis 17:10-12).

This was the beginning of a covenant — a "two-way promise." It was the beginning of a very special relationship between God and Abraham and Sarah's family. As you will note in verse 7 of that same chapter, God promises *"to be God to you and to your offspring after you."* In turn, Abraham and Sarah's family were to be God's chosen people.

Please note: No infant "chose God as his personal Lord and savior"! The infants were only eight days old when they were marked with the sign of the covenant. Consequently, we are to remember that this is how God works. God *first* chooses people and then awaits a faithful response. Like it or not, the chosen now belong to God!

Also notice that circumcision is exclusive here to men. Women were considered a part of that covenant family only by virtue of the fact that they were born or married into it.

Being "Chosen" But Not Living It

As the years passed, the descendants of Abraham continued to circumcise. They were, after all, God's chosen people. Still, there were some very dark chapters in the history of these people — now known as "the people of Israel." They turned away from God. After they had been freed by God from slavery in Egypt, they wandered in the desert of the Sinai peninsula. When "the going got rough" and they were in need, they did not turn to God. They turned to "false gods" — carved images of fake gods who would not be true to any promises — unlike The One True God. Although this may seem strange to us, how often is it today that we turn to something or someone other than God when we are truly in need?

Moses told the people of Israel that when they were ready to return to God, God would be ready to receive them. *"Return to the Lord your God"* (Deuteronomy 30:2). *"The Lord is slow to anger, and abounding in steadfast love"* (Numbers 14:18).

Is it possible to be a part of God's chosen people and not trust God? Is it possible to be a part of God's chosen people but have no faith in God? Is it possible to be a part of God's chosen people and still go against God's will? Indeed! Is it desirable? Hardly. The people were lost without God. They were circumcised; they were set apart and loved as God's people and then they turned away from God. Just imagine how that made God feel.

In the years to follow, even Jesus emphasizes this way in which God works. *"You did not choose me but I chose you"* (John 15:16).

Returning To God

When, at various points in time in their lives, the people "returned" to God, they made use of a couple of very different practices to mark that change in their lives. First was to make a sacrifice on the altar within God's Temple as a "sin offering" on their behalf. (This practice was discontinued in the first century A.D.) Another way was to be physically cleansed to mark that change. As their wrongs were as "dirt" upon their lives, so now through their actions, they would present themselves as clean. Indeed, it was a physical bath! Prior to entering the Temple or at other significant times, they would immerse themselves in a pool for cleansing. This way, they understood themselves as "acceptable" in God's sight.

When non-Jews became a part of the Jewish community, they were circumcised and required to go through a thorough cleansing bath.

John the Baptist is an excellent example of this (Mark 1). He knew of the people's ways. He knew of their need to return to God. He challenged the people to mark that change in their lives by taking one of those baths. Both Jews and non-Jews came to him. *Please note that the original language from which the Bible was translated, Greek, has the word "baptismo" as the word we read translated into English as "baptism"!* The practice of baptism was not new to John the Baptist. It was not new to Jesus. What they did with it was new.

To the dismay of the Jewish authorities, John the Baptist was expecting Jews to be cleansed as thoroughly as the non-Jews. With Jesus, baptism took on yet one more dimension.

Did those "baths" of John make the people a part of God's chosen community? Not at that time. God first chose them in circumcision. They were always to be God's. The baths were merely a way of marking a point in time when someone returned to God.

Today, every time when we do wrong and then return to God, is it necessary to make a sacrifice? Is it necessary to take a shower? Hardly. How often would we need to take such a bath? Every time we go astray from God?

5

Jesus Commands Us To Baptize

Jesus was baptized ("washed") by John (Mark 1:9-11). This marked the beginning of Jesus' public ministry. At the very end of his earthly ministry, he commanded his followers to baptize. *"Go therefore and make disciples of all nations, baptizing them in the name of the Father and of the Son and of the Holy Spirit"* (Matthew 28:19). Please note that this is *a commandment* from Jesus — not a suggestion.

The critical question for us remains: "What did Jesus *really* mean by this?" Was he asking us to continue with the practice of repeated cleansings every time we wish to be seen as acceptable in God's sight? No.

Jesus' baptism was different from John's and the baptisms that preceded. John himself made that very clear. *"I baptize you with water; but one who is more powerful than I is coming ... He will baptize you with the Holy Spirit and fire"* (Luke 3:16).

So what could this possibly be like? With regards to the "fire," we see how this is described when the Holy Spirit comes to the early Christian community as tongues of fire (after Jesus' death, resurrection and ascension) in Acts 2:3. With regards to "the Holy Spirit", this refers to how the Holy Spirit *begins* a mighty work in a person at baptism.

But how do we know the appropriate way in which to understand and practice Holy Baptism? Do you think that Jesus would have explained this to his first followers? He must have. The writer of the book of Acts *"wrote about all that Jesus did and taught from the beginning until the day when he was taken up to heaven, after giving instructions through the Holy Spirit to the apostles whom he had chosen. After his suffering he presented himself alive to them by many convincing proofs, appearing to them during forty days and speaking about the kingdom of God"* (Acts 1:1-3).

The importance of this cannot be overstated. Jesus' first followers were basically uninformed with regards to God's plan until the resurrected Jesus had made it clear for them. So then, who would be best to seek when trying to discern God's intent for baptism?

... A look to those who were closest to Jesus, his first follow-ers and the early Christian community, would serve us well.

So How Did The First Christians Practice Baptism?

All of the specific stories of baptism in the early Christian Church can be found within the book of Acts. (Please note Appendix II: "Baptisms Recorded In The Book Of Acts".)
There are a total of nine baptismal stories.
* two of people with no children (Acts 8:26-40; 9:1-19);
* three that do not exclude infants/children (Acts 2:14-42; 10:44-48; 19:1-10);
* **four include infants/children as noteworthy (Acts 8:4-7; 16:11-15; 16:31-34; 18:5-11)**!

Regarding the four that include infants/children as notewor-thy, it is important to know that your Bible in English may need some explanation. There are two words translated into English that have very significant meanings in their original languages; οικος¹ which is translated as "household" and ανδρες² which is translated as "men." Οικος appears three times. It includes one's whole family: wife, children, servants and relatives living in the house. Ανδρες appears once. It frequently denotes more or less the totality of a population. Both of these words give us *a very clear indication that infant baptism was frequently practiced among the first Christians.*

Although it would be impossible for an infant to come to be baptized on his or her own, we do hear stories of the first Chris-tians being received as entire families — most likely including infants.

Further research into the early Christian Church (from manu-scripts such as Hippolytus, Origen, and Cyprian that follow our Bible) also shows that this practice of receiving entire households was common. [Please note Appendix III: "Baptisms In The Early Church (After The Bible)."]

There are a couple other important things to note. First, women and children were usually overlooked in the Bible. As sad as it may sound, women were considered little more than pieces of property. Children simply weren't important. In the entire New Testament, John the Baptist and Jesus are the only two infants even mentioned!

Jesus taught his first followers otherwise; *"Let the little children come to me, and do not stop them; for it is to such as these that the kingdom of heaven belongs"* (Matthew 19:14). Women like Mary Magdalene, Mary the Mother of James, Salome, and others were among his closest followers.

In spite of this, we hear some very profound things regarding baptism. We hear of *"Lydia and her household"* being received into the faith (16:11-15). Lydia was a woman who could not even be circumcised! The writer of Acts must have chosen to mention this particular baptismal story because of its significance. Unlike circumcision, women are received into the faith "on equal ground" as men! The woman who would have normally been overlooked is not overlooked by God. This was a very profound and radical change!

The writer even made a point of including a story about an Ethiopian eunuch who was baptized (Acts 8:26-40). A eunuch, one who was castrated, was considered even lower than women on the social strata. In addition, Ethiopians were "one of those foreigners." Still, this person was received "on equal ground" as all others!

Can you begin to see what was happening? Baptism became God's radical way of choosing all sorts of people to be a part of God's chosen community.

How About Re-baptisms?

There is *not one* story of a re-baptism *in the name of God, the Father, Son, and Holy Spirit.* Once a part of the family, always a part of the family.

Becoming A Part Of One "Family" ("Community")

Most other references to baptism within the New Testament talk about baptism as a symbol of unity for the Church. For example, the Apostle Paul writes in Ephesians 4:5 that there is *"one Lord, one faith, one baptism, one God and Father of all."* When one is baptized, one is baptized into *one* Church "family" with God as the one "Father" (/"parent"). *"As many of you as were baptized into Christ have clothed yourselves with Christ. There is no longer Jew or Greek, there is no longer slave or free, there is no longer male and female; for all of you are one in Christ Jesus"* (Galatians 3:27-28).

What Happened To Circumcision?

In Acts 15:1-21, we read how the early Christian community was wrestling with whether it would be necessary for non-Jews to be circumcised in order to become a part of the Christian community. The early leaders in the Church came to the conclusion that it would *not* be necessary for the non-Jews to be circumcised in order officially to become a part of the Christian community.

If circumcision was not necessary, how did people become a part of the faith community? Through baptism!

They hearkened back to Jesus' words that can be found in John 3:5, *"No one can enter the kingdom of God without being born of water and Spirit."* For Jesus, "water and Spirit" means baptism. Entrance into the new kingdom or community of God is through baptism.

This makes sense when considering this within the context of circumcision and the witness of Scriptures as a whole. Just as no eight-day-old infant chose the Lord as his "personal Lord" in circumcision, so too does no eight-day-old infant choose Jesus as his "personal Lord and Savior" in baptism. *God chooses us.* We are God's. Baptism defines *"who* I am and *whose* I am" — not just "what I did."

Unlike circumcision, in baptism, God "levels the playing field." All are received equally. The baptism of Jesus *radically* shows no partiality even with respect to race, gender, nationality, or even whether the person is capable of responding to the love of God (i.e. infants in families).

Baptism now replaces circumcision. *"In him also you were circumcised with a spiritual circumcision, by putting off the body of the flesh in the circumcision of Christ; when you were buried with him in baptism, you were also raised with him through faith in the power of God, who raised him from the dead"* (Colossians 2:11-12).

The Apostle Paul And Baptism

Although the Apostle Paul primarily left the job of baptizing to others within the Christian community (1 Corinthians 1:14-17), he lived within the context of communities baptizing all ages. He presents powerful imagery in his writings of what it is like to become a part of God's family through baptism. *"He destined us for adoption as his children through Jesus Christ, according to the good pleasure of his will ..."* (Ephesians 1:5). Here again, we are reminded that being a part of the family is God's action of accepting us. What could be a more powerful image than adoption? God claims and embraces us as God's own through baptism! Babies do not choose which family into which they wish to be adopted. They are simply valued, included, and claimed. Without God, we are as orphans.

Baptism: Our Christian "Birth Mark"

We carry family surnames with us throughout our entire life. It constantly reminds us to whom we belong. Once baptized in the Christian Church, our baptism serves as the reminder that we belong to God's family — for life. As we hear in the service of

10

baptism, we have been "sealed by the Holy Spirit and marked with the cross of Christ forever."

God Awaits Our Response

Like those circumcised in the Old Testament, God first chooses us. God also gives us the freedom either to claim him or not claim him. God initiates the relationship. God waits for our response. Will we *live* as people who are a part of that family? Will we say, "Yes!"? Will we say, "No, thanks. You're not that important for me right now"? Remembering the fact that we have been baptized is a way of helping us turn and face God. Different people have different ways of making this a part of their daily lives. Some even make the sign of the cross with water pouring down over their head in the shower every morning! "... This is *who* I am and this is *whose* I am." Our faithful response is critical — if God means anything to us at all.

One's commitment to God must be renewed *daily*. It is a *daily* act of "repentance" which literally means "changing direction." Each new day, we have the opportunity to open our lives to the work of God's Spirit, receive God's forgiveness for the wrongs in our past, and follow God's direction in our lives. *"If any want to become my followers, let them deny themselves and take up their cross daily and follow me"* (Luke 9:23). *"Return to the Lord, your God, for he is gracious and merciful, slow to anger, and abounding in steadfast love."* (Joel 2:13) *"I will give them a heart to know that I am the Lord; and they shall be my people and I will be their God, for they shall return to me with their whole heart"* (Jeremiah 24:7).

A Story With Meaning For Us ...

Jesus tells the story of the "prodigal son" in Luke 15:11-32. It is a great example for us regarding baptism. In the story, a son takes his portion of the family's inheritance, turns his back on his family, squanders the inheritance and ends up returning to the Father with great shame. Instead of chastising the son for his stupidity, the Father is absolutely elated that the son has returned. He welcomes him back with open arms and throws a party.

So it is with us. God chooses us to be a part of a family — sometimes as an infant. We may turn our back on God. We may never ever have anything to do with God's family. Still, God chose us to be a part of the family. And, God still eagerly awaits our return as part of God's family. God's always there for us — with open arms.

---

1. οικος ("household"/"entire family") in Acts 16:15, 33; 18:8. *"The 'House' as a Group in the Structure of the Christian Community. Primitive Christianity structured its congregations in families, groups and 'houses.' The house was both a fellowship and a place of meeting. It is explicitly emphasized that the conversion of a man leads his whole family to the faith; this would include wife, children, servants, and relatives living in the house. The use of οικος for 'house,' 'family,' is found elsewhere in primitive Christianity."* Otto Michel, "οικος," in *Theological Dictionary of the New Testament*, gen. ed. Gerhard Friedrich (Grand Rapids: Eerdmans, 1967), vol. 5, p. 130.

2. ανδρες ("men") in Acts 8:12b. Its root is ανηρ. *"In the NT ανηρ is most common in the Hellenistic Luke. ... ανδρες frequently denotes more or less the totality of population."* Albrecht Oepke, "ανδρες," in *Theological Dictionary of the New Testament*, gen. ed. Gerhard Friedrich (Grand Rapids: Eerdmans, 1967), vol. 1, p. 362.

Appendix I:
Frequently Asked Questions

Isn't baptism an "outward sign of an inward conversion"?

- To the credit of those who hold to this view, it is incredibly important that a deeper level of commitment be "named" and owned by those who have truly been "transformed" by the gospel of Jesus Christ. Still, we must honestly discern if baptism was truly intended as a means to that end. When looking at the witness of the Scriptures as a whole, this may have been true of the adults who converted to Christianity — but certainly not the children and infants received into the community through baptism.

If my baby is baptized, will my baby be going to heaven?

- The assurance of salvation comes only when the promises in baptism are claimed in faith. *Faith* is the critical "component." *"For by grace you have been saved through faith, and this is not your own doing; it is the gift of God"* (Ephesians 2:8). Baptism is not a mystical "after-life insurance" policy.

Isn't it important for my children to make their own "decisions"?

- Yes, but no parent is going to wait until his/her children are eighteen years old before telling them to brush their teeth. Parents naturally share family values and beliefs. Like it or not, children, once older, will make decisions regarding "owning" any of those things. To withhold important things from children when they need it the most is not beneficial for them. At least after a number of years within the Christian community, a person is capable of making an informed decision regarding Christianity as opposed to an absolutely uninformed one. Free thinking should be allowed and even encouraged within the Church. The Church does not need to serve as a "brain-washing" institution. If a parent truly believes it, why wait until the children are "of age" to tell them that God loves them and we know that because of Jesus Christ?

What if something happens to my child before he or she is really capable of understanding Christianity and having faith?

- Remember that faith is more than a system of beliefs to carry in your head. It is *trusting in God*. Matthew 18:3 reads, *"Unless you change and become like children, you will never enter the kingdom of heaven."* Who's more trusting than a child? Think of how much you love your child. Now think of how much more God, who created your child, must love your child! There is no need to worry.

I didn't have my child baptized as an infant. How about having a private baptism?

- Although a private baptism is acceptable, it is not preferable. Why? Because one is becoming part of a family. Could you imagine being adopted into a family and not even being in their presence? Why not allow for the family to participate and celebrate in this most wonderful event as well? It may be a bit embarrassing to you since your child was not baptized as an infant. Don't worry about it! Simply know that you have a community of people just waiting to celebrate a baptism with you. It is a wonderful event to celebrate — not a shameful one!

Isn't it important for baptism to involve my decision?

- God chooses us. We respond. God gets the credit of the miracle of faith — not us. Jesus says in John 15:16, *"You did not choose me but I chose you."* Each new day of our Christian life is an opportunity for us to respond to that call.

I've just returned to the Christian faith. I would like a special way to mark my change in direction and increased commitment. How about baptism?

- Although the baptism of John the Baptist may have been repeated, there is no account of a re-baptism in the name of God, the Father, Son, and Holy Spirit once Jesus established the Church. This is because baptism became the means for incorporation into the community with Jesus' first followers. It takes

14

the place of circumcision. If you would like to mark this significant point in time, a public affirmation (saying "Yes!") to your
baptism is very appropriate — possibly during the worship service. You can talk with the pastor about this. You can also keep
in mind the words of John the Baptist in Luke 3:8: *"Bear fruits
worthy of repentance."* In other words, have something to show
for the change in your life. Do more than just splash around
some water. Worship God among God's people. Be engaged in
acts of kindness and mercy. Give of your time, talents, and pos-
sessions to the work of God's kingdom!

Why circumcise today?

- Although there is clearly no Christian reason for the current practice of circumcision, many still follow the practice. In years past,
the medical profession has advocated the practice for hygienic
purposes. More recently, these reasons have been called into
question. Consult your physician for making an informed decision.

What about immersion verses "sprinkling"?

- Church history is helpful here. When the church originated in
the warm climate of the Middle East, immersion baptism was
the preferred means. (In some cases, variations on this were practiced.*) When it expanded into parts of Europe, immersion became a bit of a problem in the winter! Consequently, the practice of "sprinkling" emerged. Immersion is great. For us, both
practices are acceptable. Do you think God would really con-
demn a person simply because the *quantity* of water "didn't meet
specifications"?

---

* *"According to Didache, this ought if possible to take place in "living [i.e.,
flowing] water," presumably by immersion. In the absence of a stream, how-
ever, it was acceptable to use standing water and even to 'pour water on the
head.'"* Williston Walker, Richard A. Norris, David W. Lotz, and Robert T.
Handy, *A History of the Christian Church* (New York: Charles Scribner's
Sons, 1985), p. 105.

Appendix II:
Baptisms Recorded In The Book Of Acts

2:14-42   3,000 in Jerusalem

8:4-17   Simon the magician *and the men and women*[2] of Samaria
Were baptized in the name of Jesus and then later received the Holy Spirit through the laying on of hands.

8:26-40   Ethiopian eunuch
Not Jewish. Not even male or female!

9:1-19   Saul (Paul)

10:44-48   Gentiles in Caesarea
Received the Holy Spirit and then were baptized "in the name of Jesus Christ."

16:11-15   Lydia *and her household*[1]
"when she and her household were baptized ..."

16:31-34   Jailer at Philippi *and his entire family*[1]
"he and his entire family were baptized"

18:5-11   Crispus, *all his household*[1], many of the Corinthians
"Crispus, the official of the synagogue, became a believer in the Lord, together with all his household; and many of the Corinthians who heard Paul became believers and were baptized."

19:1-10   Some disciples in Ephesus
Were baptized in "the baptism of John" and then later baptized "in the name of the Lord Jesus."

22:6-16 Paul's conversion/baptism story retold

1. οικος ("household"/"entire family") in Acts 16:15, 33; 18:8. *"The 'House' as a Group in the Structure of the Christian Community. Primitive Christianity structured its congregations in families, groups and 'houses.' The house was both a fellowship and a place of meeting.* **It is explicitly emphasized that the conversion of a man leads his whole family to the faith; this would include wife, children, servants and relatives living in the house.** *The use of* οικος *for 'house,' 'family,' is found elsewhere in primitive Christianity."* Otto Michel, "οικος," in *Theological Dictionary of the New Testament*, gen. ed. Gerhard Friedrich (Grand Rapids: Eerdmans, 1967), vol. 5, p. 130.

2. ανδρες ("men") in Acts 8:12b. Its root is ανηρ. *"In the NT* ανηρ *is most common in the Hellenistic Luke ...* ανδρες *frequently denotes more or less the totality of population."* Albrecht Oepke, "ανδρες," in *Theological Dictionary of the New Testament*, gen. ed. Gerhard Friedrich (Grand Rapids: Eerdmans, 1967), vol. 1, p. 362.

17

Appendix III:
Baptisms In The Early Church
(After The Bible)

Hippolytus (3rd Century)

"They were then taken by a deacon into the water — infants (for whom their parents spoke) and children first ..."

Apostolic Tradition 20-22 quoted by Williston Walker, Richard A. Norris, David W. Lotz, and Robert T. Handy, *A History of the Christian Church* (New York: Charles Scribner's Sons, 1985), p. 106.

Origen (3rd Century)

"In the writings of Origen ... the custom of infant baptism was taken to be of apostolic origin. He maintained that there was 'a tradition of the church from the apostles' to administer baptism also to infants."

Jarislav Pelikan, *The Christian Tradition: A History of the Development of Doctrine*, Vol. 1: *The Emergence of the Catholic Tradition* (Chicago: The University of Chicago Press, 1973), pp. 290-291.

Cyprian (3rd Century)

"It had apparently been a custom for some parts of the church to baptize infants on the eighth day after their birth, but Cyprian insisted that this was too long to wait."

Ibid., p. 291.

Appendix IV:
Martin Luther On Baptism
("The Small Catechism")

1. What is Baptism?
Answer: Baptism is not simply plain water. Instead it is water used according to God's command and connected with God's Word.

What then is this Word of God?
Answer: Where our Lord Jesus Christ says in Matthew 28:19, *"Go therefore and make disciples of all nations, baptizing them in the name of the Father and of the Son and of the Holy Spirit."*

2. What gifts or benefits does Baptism grant?
Answer: It brings about forgiveness of sins, redeems from death and the devil, and gives eternal salvation to all who believe it, as the Word and promise of God declare.

What is this Word and promise of God?
Answer: Where our Lord Jesus Christ says in Mark 16:16, *"The one who believes and is baptized will be saved; but the one who does not believe will be condemned."*

3. How can water do such great things?
Answer: Clearly the water does not do it, but the Word of God, which is with, in, and among the water, and faith, which trusts this Word of God in the water. For without the Word of God the water is plain water and not a baptism, but with the Word of God it is a baptism, that is, a grace-filled water of life and a "bath of the new birth in the Holy Spirit." As St. Paul says to

Titus in 3:5-8, *"He saved us, not because of any works of righteousness that we had done, but according to his mercy, through the water of rebirth and renewal by the Holy Spirit. This Spirit he poured out on us richly through Jesus Christ our Savior, so that, having been justified by his grace, we might become heirs according to the hope of eternal life. The saying is sure."*

4. What then is the significance of such a baptism with water?

Answer: It signifies that daily the old person in us with all our sins and evil desires is to be drowned through sorrow for sin and repentance, and that daily a new person is to come forth and rise up to live before God in righteousness and purity forever.

Where is this written?

Answer: Saint Paul says in Romans 6:3-4, *"Do you not know that all of us who have been baptized into Christ Jesus were baptized into his death? Therefore we have been buried with him by baptism into death, so that, just as Christ was raised from the dead by the glory of the Father, so we too might walk in newness of life."*

A Contemporary Translation of Luther's Small Catechism: Incorporating texts from the New Revised Standard Version Bible and Lutheran Book of Worship, Translation and Introduction by Timothy J. Wengert (Minneapolis: Augsburg, 1994), pp. 41-43.